The Magical Amulets

of the

Ancient Sages

AND

Bibliotheca Necromantica

The Magical Amulets of the Ancient Sages and Bibliotheca Necromantica
by Johannes Trithemius
Translation and Introduction Copyright © 2023 Robert Nixon
ISBN 978-1-914166-42-6 (Hardcover)
ISBN 978-1-914166-43-3 (Softcover)
ISBN 978-1-914166-41-9 (Digital)

Published by Hadean Press
West Yorkshire
www.hadeanpress.com

A catalogue for this title is available from the British Library.

Robert Nixon has asserted his moral right to be identified as the author of this work.

Johannes Trithemius

The Magical Amulets
of the
Ancient Sages

AND

Bibliotheca Necromantica

TRANSLATED BY
Fr. Robert Nixon, OSB

Contents

Translator's Introduction

ohannes Trithemius (1462–1515), described as 'a man of peerless intelligence, and a radiant beam of all erudition in his own age, most fertile though it was in extremely learned men',[1] was a German Benedictine monk and abbot, who possessed profound and penetrating knowledge in a bewildering variety of disciplines. His best-known works today are his *Polygraphia* and *Steganographia*. These curious and widely studied tomes can be read literally as treatises on angelic magic, yet they also function as extraordinarily complex examples of sophisticated cryptography. His volumes on the *Illustrious Writers of the Church* and the *Illustrious Persons of the Benedictine Order* continue to be authoritative reference books for scholars of ecclesiastical and monastic history. His devout musings on the life of St. Anne, the mother of the Blessed Virgin Mary, were of central importance in promoting popular devotion to that saint. He also wrote on secular history, canon law, witchcraft, and angelic theology. Indeed, his works encompass virtually the entire spectrum of early Renaissance

---

1 Wolfgang Ernst Heidel, 'Epistola Dedicatoria Damiano Hartardo', in Johannes Trithemius, *Steganographia Vindicata, Reserata et Illustrata* (Nuremberg: Johannes Freidrich Rüdiger, 1721).

learning, and establish him as a most formidable and accomplished polymath. His students included both Cornelius Agrippa and Paracelsus, and he was a close friend of the 'real-life' Faust (i.e. Johann Fust, a printer, money-lender, and business partner of Gutenberg). He served as a respected consultant and confidante on occult matters to the imperial court and to many of the nobles of Germany.

Trithemius was born in 1462 in Trittenheim, a town on the banks of the Moselle River in the diocese of Trier. It is from this town that he received his cognomen. His father passed away while he was an infant, and (as a result of various domestic hardships, including harsh beatings from his stepfather) the young Johannes was compelled to pursue his beloved literary studies under the cover of secrecy. It is related that at night, when all members of his household had fallen asleep, he would stealthily creep out of his house to visit a friend, who would instruct him in reading and writing. His progress was so rapid that within the space of a month of commencing his studies he had thoroughly mastered the art of reading vernacular texts.[2]

In 1482, inspired by an ardent desire to advance his education, he fled from his family home, travelling first to Trier and then to Heidelberg. But one night he was caught outside in a heavy snowstorm, in the vicinity of the Benedictine abbey at Sponheim. He sought refuge in that monastery, and it was there that he came to

---

2 Wolfgang Ernst Heidel, 'Vita Johannis Trithemii', in Johannes Trithemius, *Steganographia Vindicata, Reserata et Illustrata* (Nuremberg: Johannes Friedrich Rüdiger, 1721), p. 2.

embrace the monastic life,[3] taking the black habit of the Order of St. Benedict on the day of his twentieth birthday.[4] Within approximately a year of his admission as a novice monk, he was elected abbot of the same monastery. Almost incredibly, his election as head of the community followed the date of his profession by only eight months and seven days.[5] Such a rapid ascent to ecclesiastical leadership is virtually unprecedented, especially for a person of poor and obscure origins and with no formal education.[6] As to how Trithemius achieved this feat, one may only speculate.

During his tenure as abbot, he worked vigorously to improve the temporal, intellectual and spiritual well-being of the monastery, particularly by enriching and expanding its library to include many rare and curious volumes of arcane lore.[7] However, in 1506 he departed

---

3 Heidel, 'Vita Trithemii', p. 3.

4 Johannes Duraclus, 'Pinax sive Index Lucubrationum Joannis Trithemii', in Johannes Trithemius, *Libri Polygraphiae VI* (Cologne: Johannes Birkmann & Werner Richwin, 1564), p. 4.

5 Heidel, 'Vita Trithemii', p. 13.

6 St. Bernard of Clairvaux was also elected abbot of his monastery a mere year after his entry into the novitiate. But his case was very different from that of Trithemius—for Bernard was from a wealthy, illustrious and powerful family, and entered the monastery with a group of thirty other friends and relatives of his, who (by sheer numbers) would have quickly gained dominance in the community.

7 It is reported that when Trithemius first arrived, the monastery's library consisted of a mere forty volumes, but by the time he departed, he had acquired over 2,000 books.

from Sponheim, leaving (as he himself testifies) of his own free well, in response to 'injuries done to him by the envious',[8] and apparently under a cloud of suspicion for his interest in the occult arts. Shortly after this, he accepted the abbacy of the much smaller St. James Abbey in Würzburg, occupying this position for the remainder of his earthly life. His death in 1516 was, according to contemporary reports, received 'with mourning and weeping by all learned persons, and indeed by the emperor himself and many princes'.[9]

The work presented here is a translation (for the first time in English) of a Latin text, entitled *Veterum Sophorum Sigilla et Imagines Magicae* (literally, *Magical Sigils and Images of the Ancient Sages*). It was not published by Trithemius during his lifetime, but copied from his extant manuscripts by Friedrich Roth-Scholtz, and brought to light by him in 1732.[10] In this context, the attribution to Trithemius is necessarily somewhat uncertain and ambiguous—especially since the text is essentially a compilation of writings from other, and supposedly more ancient, authorities, rather than a newly composed or unified book in itself.[11] Nevertheless,

---

8 Johannes Trithemius, 'Chronicon Monasterii Sancti Jacobi', in Johannes Trithemius, *Opera Pia et Spirituales* (Mainz: Johannes Albinus, 1605), p. 15.

9 Trithemius, 'Chronicon Monasterii Sancti Jacobi', p. 17.

10 Johannes Trithemius, *Veterum Sophorum Sigilla et Imagines Magicae* (Herrnstadt: Friedrich Roth-Scholtz, 1732).

11 This fact that it is a composite work is reflected in the repetition of the descriptions of a number of amulets in various different locations.

Roth-Scholtz was a reliable and conscientious scholar, and there seems little reason to doubt either his veracity or his judgment in this matter.

This fascinating work presents five tracts, attributed respectively to the Archangel Raphael, the ancient sage Chael, Hermes Trismegistus, Thetel (a legendary Hebrew physician), and King Solomon. Of course, these authorial attributions are entirely pseudepigraphical, but nevertheless typical of those found in grimoires and magical treatises of the late Middle Ages and early Renaissance. Each of these tracts describes the various properties and potencies believed to be possessed by various images carved from stone. These images or amulets could either be set in rings, or worn around the neck, or simply carried about one's person. In certain instances, they are to be placed under a pillow while sleeping, or brought into contact with the subject whom one wishes to enchant, or used in some other particular way.

The collection of tracts attest to a belief in the intimate connection and mutual influence of physical and spiritual realities. Such a belief, which springs from and is justified by the intelligent and sensitive observation of the influence of objects upon spirit and of spirit upon objects, seems to be wholly compatible with lived, quotidian human experience, as well as the wisdom of the ancient sages of virtually all lands and cultures.

For the physical objects by which we are surrounded, and particularly those which we wear on our own persons, have an undeniable spiritual and psychological effect, both on ourselves and on others. Such a proposition is hardly likely to be disputed in principle, even by the most doctrinaire scientific materialist; and the extensive employment of sacred images and holy relics within the Catholic faith stems from recognition of the truth of this principle. One could argue that what Trithemius and/or the original authors of the tracts are doing is simply systematically recording and cataloguing such effects, and offering ways in which they may be deliberately and advantageously employed.

Of course, a certain number of descriptions of amulets promise results which are patently impossible and implausible, such as invisibility; however, these instances may be read as serving as important 'hermeneutic clues' or interpretative monitions for the reader. Such cases are effective reminders that the promised effects should never be understood in an overly simplistic or literal way. For example, an amulet which is said to bring 'success in conflicts' to its bearer should not be understood as guaranteeing such success in any literal or automatic sense, as if it is expected to function as a direct causal agent. Rather, its immediate effect may be an increase in confidence, courage, or determination for the person who wears or carries it; and this, in turn, may increase the probability of their success in any conflicts in which they happen to find themselves involved.

That, of course, is only one extremely simple case, offered for the purpose of the illustration of a principle. More complex images (such as many of those described herein) may have an array of subtle spiritual and psychological effects both on those who wear them and those who perceive them—which, in turn, may precipitate a multitude of possible (and relatively predictable) behavioral outcomes. For, as Jung observes, 'there are as many archetypes as there are situations in life'. These archetypal images are 'engraved into our psychic constitution', and are each 'accompanied by a type of perception and action'.[12]

In the final section of the work, Trithemius offers his own more mystical and theological rationale for the efficacy of these amulets:

> It is to be noted that the reason [for their effects] is *not* any quality of the materials from which they are made, nor does it originate from some property arising from the totality of their form and substance. Rather the reason is purely Divine, or magical. This indicates that it originates from some more sublime and hidden Cause, which may be appropriately termed a spiritual bond or conduit. For by the mediation of this hidden Cause, the physical and spiritual realms (which are far removed from each other in substance and nature) are brought into connection. [13]

---

12 C.G. Jung, *The Archetypes and the Collective Unconscious*, trans. R.F.C. Hull (London: Routledge, 2014), p. 48.

13 Trithemius, *Veterum Sophorum Sigilla*, pp. 43–44.

In this context, there is no essential philosophical incongruity between the sincerity of the professed faith of Trithemius and his exploration and employment of the hidden ('occult') connections between symbols and reality, and the realms of matter and of spirit.

Also included in this volume is an extensive catalogue of books on necromancy, magic, and divination compiled by Trithemius, and given the title of *Bibliotheca Necromantica* by the present translator. It was originally included in his *Antipalus Maleficiorum (The Foe of Sorceries)*, a compendious study of witchcraft written at the behest of Joachim, the Marquis of Brandenburg, in 1508.[14] A number of the volumes mentioned (such as the *Clavicula Salomonis, Picatrix*, and the *Heptameron* of Peter of Albano) are well-known and readily available today, but most remain obscure and unknown—perhaps to be discovered someday by an enterprising and diligent scholar. This remarkable catalogue of Trithemius offers a fascinating insight into the nature, diversity and sheer quantity of works of occult literature which were in underground circulation

---

14 The *Antipalus Maleficiorum* appeared in print in a single-volume edition published in Mainz in 1605 by Balthasar Lippius, and was also included in a compendium of the collected of works of Trithemius compiled by Joannes Busaeus in the same year. References to a 1555 Ingolstadt edition occur in many secondary sources, but this appears to be the result of confusion with a German-language edition of his *Antwort auff acht Fragstuck* (*'Answers to Eight Questions'*), which also treats the subject of witchcraft and sorcery. See Johannes Trithemius, *Antwort auff acht Fragstuck* (Ingolstadt: Alexander and Samuel Weissenhorn, 1555).

in Europe (either in print or in manuscript) in the early sixteenth century. While many references are made to this list in the secondary literature, a complete English translation of it has not yet been made available.

It remains up to the intrepid reader to experiment with the diverse amulets described in these pages, and to determine their effectiveness for themselves; and, if they have the inclination and opportunity, to attempt to locate or identify the intriguing works referred to in the *Bibliotheca Necromantica*. In these endeavors, as in all spiritual and intellectual pursuits, may the seeker of higher and hidden truths be confident that 'the one who asks always receives, and the one who seeks always finds.'[15]

Fr. Robert Nixon, OSB,
Abbey of the Most Holy Trinity,
New Norcia

---

15 Matthew 7:8.

A Note on the Translation

In preparing this translation, the primary consideration has been fidelity to the intended sense of the original text. An effort has also been made to produce a readable and acceptably idiomatic English rendition.

Accordingly, very long sentences in Latin have often been divided into several English sentences. Minor typographical and orthographical errors and inconsistencies in the original have mostly been corrected without comment, with footnotes added only where there is a genuine ambiguity as to the meaning. Square brackets [ ] signify editorial insertions made to clarify or complete the sense of the original text. Rounded brackets ( ) are used as punctuation marks to indicate parenthetical phrases or comments which are part of the original text.

It is important to note that the varieties of stones which are named in these texts do not necessarily match exactly with their modern gemological definitions (which are based on the identification of chemical composition, refractive index, specific gravity, etc.). During the Middle Ages and in the times of Trithemius, stones were classified principally according to their visible and perceptible properties, such as color, texture, luster, and density. For this reason, the names of various stones should be understood as referring only to these visible and perceptible properties, rather than serving to identify a specific chemical composition. Thus, any gemstone of a rich red color (ruby, almandine garnet, red spinel, etc.) could be validly classified as a 'ruby', and any gemstone of a green color (emerald, green sapphire, tsavorite, or demantoid garnet, etc.) could be considered an 'emerald'.

Prayer of Trithemius to his Guardian Angel

My protecting Angel and guardian Spirit!

By thy invisible presence, thou hast faithfully shielded me from the attacks of evil spirits and malicious demons. Thou hast annulled their powers to harm me, and thou hast graciously bestowed upon me the strength and courage to resist all their nefarious designs.

I confess that I am but a fragile and weak human being, capricious and unstable as the waves of the ocean—who, without thy precious and potent succor and subvention, would not be able to evade or withstand the multitudinous snares and deceptions with which my spiritual and earthly foes ceaselessly assault and assail me.

Therefore, O radiant Angel and supernal guardian of my soul, assist me with thy benevolent goodness, fortify me with thy invincible strength, and protect me under the tutelary shadow of thy golden pinions. Be thou my constant and familiar companion during my perilous exile in this earthly valley of tears. And when at last my immortal soul is released from the prison of the body, defend it from the clutches of all malevolent demons; and guide it safely, by virtue of thy most pure and refulgent light, unto the celestial shores of

Heavenly eternity—there to dwell forever and ever in the infinite and everlasting bliss of Paradise! Amen.

Johannes Trithemius,
Abbot of Sponheim, 1495.[16]

16 See Johannes Trithemius, 'Orationes ad Sanctos', in *Paralipomena Opusculorum Petri Blesensis, Et Joannis Trithemii, Aliorumque Nuper In Typographeo Moguntino editorum,* (Mainz: Balthasar Lippius, 1605), pp. 735–738. The text given above is an abridgement of the original.

The Magical Amulets
of the Ancient Sages

The Amulets of the Archangel Raphael

If the image of a beautiful dragon is fashioned out of ruby, or another rubicund gemstone of a similar nature, you shall find that it has the power of increasing for the person who bears it their prosperity in the goods and riches of this world. It also makes the one who possesses it both happy and healthy.

If an image of a falcon is fashioned from topaz, it shall have the effect of procuring for its bearer the good-will of monarchs, rulers, and other eminent persons.

If the likeness of an astrolabe[17] is carved out of granite, its power will be to produce and preserve health in the person who carries it or wears it. It shall also protect its bearer from all illness and adversities whilst on a journey.

If the image of an ass is made from chrysolite, it shall convey to its possessor the ability to predict and foretell the future (to the extent to which human frailty is able to do this; for indeed, to predict the future with absolute assurance and truth is the prerogative of the Divinity alone.)

If the likeness of the head of a bearded man is carved out of sapphire, it shall have the power to heal all injuries. It shall also be able to liberate the person who possesses it, either from infirmities and illness, or from prison, or from afflictions and annoyances of any other kinds. Such an amulet is a regal token, and it procures for its bearer high dignities and honors, and leads to their elevation to an exalted station.

---

17 An astrolabe was a kind of ancient astronomical device, still in use in the time of Trithemius. Smaller astrolabes often resembled compasses or pocket watches in design. Larger ones resembled globes.

If the form of a frog is fashioned out of beryl, it shall have the capacity to bring about the reconciliation of enemies. It shall produce friendship and peace amongst people, and help to resolve discords and disputes.

If the head of a camel, as well as the heads of two goats, positioned within the branches of a myrtle tree, are carved into an onyx, such an amulet shall have the power of summoning, congregating and constraining demons of all varieties. If anyone should carry or wear such an amulet while they sleep, they shall experience vivid dreams of a most marvelous and awe-inspiring nature.

If the likeness of a vulture is fashioned out of chrysolite, it shall confer to its possessor the power of restraining and congregating demonic entities. If it is placed in any location, it shall defend that location from all evil spirits, and also expel any evil spirits which may already abide there. Such an amulet will render demons obedient to the person who carries it.

The form of a bat, carved out of heliodor,[18] shall impart to the person who carries or wears it the power to resist the assaults, temptations, and deceptions of all demonic entities.

If the image of a man holding some beautiful object in his hand is fashioned out of carnelian, it shall render the one who wears it immune to the loss of blood. It shall also lead them to the attainment of honors and prestige.

If the form of a lion or of an archer is carved from any type of stone, it will confer immunity to poisons. Such an amulet shall also liberate its possessor from fevers.

If the image of a man armed with a bow and arrow is fashioned out of opal, it will protect the one who carries it from all evil. It shall similarly protect whatever location such a person abides in from all manner of harm and disaster.

---

18 Yellow or golden beryl.

The figure of a bull fashioned out of green quartz is said to help its bearers by making efficacious any works of wizardry or magic which they may perform. It shall also assist them in gaining favor from their masters or superiors.

The figure of a hoopoe bird with a dragonwort plant before it, carved out of beryl, shall impart to its possessor the ability to invoke all aquatic spirits. Furthermore, it provides its bearer with the authority to compel such spirits to speak, and to give truthful answers to any questions posed to them.

The image of a human being with his right hand raised towards Heaven, if sculpted out of chalcedony, shall furnish its bearer with successful results in all disputes in civil law. It will also assist the person who possesses it to make safe journeys, and shall protect them from all harm and injury.

If the name of God[19] is engraved into a thunderstone, it shall protect the place in which it is located from storms and tempests. For those who carry such a stone with them, it shall ensure victory against their enemies.

The form of a bear carved out of amethyst has the power of putting demons to flight. Such an amulet will also protect its bearer from the harmful effects of intoxication and drunkenness.

The image of a human being fashioned from a lodestone[20] will ensure victory in battles to whosoever bears it.

---

19 Presumably the Tetragrammaton.

20 A naturally occurring magnet.

The Amulets of Chael the Sage

The most ancient sage Chael was one of the grandsons of the patriarch Israel. While he was alone in the desert, he observed carefully the courses and arrangements of the stars and the planets, and fashioned images and figurations based upon them. Through mystical insights and practical experience, he came to be profoundly knowledgeable of the various potencies and virtues of these amulets, and compiled this information in a treatise for the benefit of future generations. It is from this treatise that the following details are taken.

May God be blessed, who has granted such powers to these mystic figures for the benefit and healing of humankind! (These words are found at the beginning of the treatise of Chael.)

[The first of the amulets of Chael consists of] the figure of a man sitting behind a plough, with a long beard and a long, supercilious face. There are to be four smaller figures of human beings lying upon the neck of the larger figure. And the larger figure is to hold in one hand a fox, and in the other hand a vulture. Now, if such an image is carved out of stone and worn around the neck, the person who wears it shall be successful in all plantings and sowings which they undertake. It is also useful for finding hidden treasure. For if you place such an amulet in your bed, when you sleep the location of the treasure will be revealed to you in a dream.

There is another power possessed by this type of amulet, namely of relieving the sicknesses and ailments of animals. In order to achieve this result, the amulet should be washed in water, and the water then given to the beasts to drink.

This variety of amulet should be sculpted on the day and hour of the planet Venus.[21]

[The second amulet of Chael is] a figure of a man having a shield suspended from his neck, a helmet on his head and a sword in his hand, and trampling a serpent under his feet. If such a figure is sculpted from red jasper and hung around the neck, it imparts the ability to defeat any foe in battle. It is especially effective if it is fashioned on the day of Mars.[22]

---

21 I.e., at the first hour of the day (beginning at sunrise, varying by location and time of year), on a Friday.

22 I.e., Tuesday.

The image of a horse with a crocodile lying upon its back, if sculpted from jacinth,[23] imparts numerous benefits to the one who possesses it. It shall make them victorious in all civil disputes, and also render them popular and lovable. Such an amulet should be set in gold; for if set in that metal, its potency is greatly enhanced.

Another powerful amulet consists of the figure of a seated man with a woman standing before him. The hair of the woman should be hanging loosely down to her waist, while the eyes of the man should be gazing upwards to the sky. If such an amulet is carved out of carnelian, whoever touches it shall be inspired to feel goodwill [towards the one who possesses the amulet]. It should be well polished with ambergris and turpentine, to enhance its effectiveness.

The figure of a horse, excited and foaming at the mouth, upon which a black man is seated with a sceptre in his hand, if fashioned from hematite,[24] imparts to its possessor the faculty of ruling others. It is also able to restore to its owner any lost favor or popularity. It should be set in a ring of equal portions of gold and silver.

---

23 I.e., red, orange or yellow zircon.

24 A crystalline form of iron oxide.

If the figure of a man holding a lighted candle in his hand is carved out of chrysolite, it has the effect of causing the one who carries it to become wealthy. Such an amulet should be set only in the purest gold.

Demons, lunatics and those afflicted by frenzy may be effectively restrained through the power of a stone amulet in the form of either a deer, or a hunter, or a dog, or a rabbit.

An amulet in the form of a woman having a bird in one hand and a fish in the other imparts to its owner success in capturing both fish and birds. It is best for this type of amulet to be set in silver.

A figure of a beast having the rear parts of a horse and the front parts of a goat may be sculpted from any kind of stone. It will give to its possessor good fortune in looking after and taming animals of all kinds. It is most potent when set in lead.

Success in hunting may be procured by carrying an image of a woman sitting upon a horse with a trumpet in her hand. The same effect may be obtained by an image of a soldier running, with a horn suspended from his neck, and a tree in front of him. Both of these amulets may be carved from a stone of any kind.

The figure of a kneeling man with his eyes turned upwards and holding a garment in his hand, if carved in any variety of stone, will impart to whoever carries it good fortune and prosperity in buying and selling things of any kind.

The figure of a scorpion and an archer fighting amongst themselves, if carved out of any stone, has the power of reconciling those who are hostile towards each other, and making enemies become friends. Such an amulet should be set in silver.

If you carry with you an image of a vulture with an olive branch in its beak, fashioned in pyrite and set in a silver ring, you shall receive invitations to many feasts and parties. It will cause all to regard you with admiration and respect.

The figure of a beast which is a half-and-half combination of a ram and a lion, if made from any precious gemstone, will reconcile people who are in conflict. Simply touch both persons with this amulet, and they shall be reconciled and be drawn into harmony with each other. It should be set in a ring of silver.

A potent amulet is the figure of a creature with the likeness of a human woman in its upper portions and the likeness of a fish in its lower portions, holding a mirror in one hand and a branch of hyacinth in the other. Such an amulet should be sculpted from jacinth, set in a gold ring, and worn upon the finger of its owner. If the ring is turned on the finger so that the figure faces inwards—that is, towards the palm of the hand—and the hand then closed upon itself, it shall render the wearer invisible to others.

An amulet of a basilisk,[25] whose upper portion is in the form of a woman and whose lower body is that of a serpent, if carved from any precious stone, has the power of repelling attacks from all malignant and venomous creatures.

---

25 A kind of mythical serpent, reputed to have the ability to kill by its glance.

The figure of a basilisk with the head of a man, fighting with a dragon, carved out of carnelian and worn around the neck, gives to the one who wears it the power of overcoming all beasts, both terrestrial and aquatic.

The figure of a man of a bloated or inflated appearance together with another man, well-dressed and holding in one hand a chalice and in the other a branch of a tree, has the power to relieve all fevers if a person carries it with them for three consecutive days. This amulet is to be sculpted from agate.

The form of a man with the head of an ox and the feet of an eagle may be carved from any variety of stone. As long as you carry this figure with you, no person will speak badly of you.

The figure of a man kneeling, with his gaze turned upwards and holding a garment in his hands, if fashioned from turquoise, will procure for its possessor success in buying and selling.[26]

An amulet of a scorpion and an archer engaged in combat may be carved from any stone. If it is set into a ring of iron, and then impressed into wax, it shall generate immediate conflict and discord between whomever you touch with it.[27]

The figure of an animal consisting of a half-and-half combination of an ox and a ram, when carved from any variety of stone and set in a ring of silver, will instantly make those you touch with it come into agreement and harmony.

---

26 The description of this amulet is virtually identical to one mentioned a little earlier in this same tract. The earlier description indicates that any variety of stone may be used.

27 An amulet of the same kind is mentioned earlier, with the power of resolving conflicts. However, in that case it was set in silver, whereas in this case it is to be set in iron.

An amulet depicting a creature with the form of a woman in its upper portions and a fish in its lower portions, and holding a mirror in one hand and the branch of a tree in the other, has the power of making its possessor invisible. It should be carved from jacinth, and set in a ring of gold. To achieve the effect of invisibility, the amulet should be covered with wax, and then the ring turned in such a way that the image faces the palm of the hand.[28]

The figure of a man ploughing, with the hand of the Lord appearing above him and a star shining in the sky near him, will protect the one who carries it from all ill effects of storms and tempests. It will also ensure that any crops cultivated by its owner shall not perish. It may be carved out of any variety of stone.

Another powerful amulet is the figure of a young man having a crown on his head and seated upon a throne. This throne should have four legs, with four men underneath it, each holding one of the legs. The one sitting upon the throne should have one of his hands raised to Heaven. This amulet should be fashioned

---

28 This is virtually identical with an amulet described a little earlier.

from white jacinth,[29] and set in a ring of silver, the weight of the metal of which should be equal to that of the stone. [When the amulet is being set into such a ring,] a little mastic and turpentine should be placed underneath it. The one who possesses such an amulet, and bears it with them in an open and visible manner, will obtain whatsoever they ask for from kings and princes.

Anyone who carries with themselves the image of a serpent with a human being and a raven both seated upon his back, carved out of any kind of stone, will be prosperous in all matters. They will also become prudent and astute.

A particularly useful amulet is the figure of a man standing upon a dragon and holding a sword in his hand, sculpted from hematite and set in a ring of lead. The one who wears such an amulet will have authority to command all subterranean spirits. These spirits, when summoned by a spell, will reveal any treasures

---

29 As noted earlier, jacinth is a kind of red, orange or yellow zircon. However, it seems unlikely that the author means here what is now called 'white zircon', which is a clear, diamond-like and somewhat brittle gemstone. It seems more likely that any kind of white crystalline stone (such as white quartz) is meant.

buried in the earth, and give truthful instructions on how these may be recovered.

The figure of a standing man, wearing a breastplate, with a helmet upon his head and an unsheathed sword in his hand, may be carved from any stone, and should be set in a ring of iron. The weight of the metal of the ring should be somewhat less than that of the stone. None shall be able to defeat in battle whosoever wears such a ring!

The image of a long-faced, bearded man with a supercilious expression and sitting upon a plough between two bulls, when carved from any stone, possesses a diversity of powers. Whoever carries with them such an amulet will be successful in all plantings and agricultural endeavors. They shall also enjoy good fortune in finding treasures, and in fighting. Moreover, they will be able to make enemies become friends, and will soon recover from whatever infirmities afflict them.

This amulet also has the ability to put serpents to flight, if its face is displayed to them. It can be used to cure those suffering from fits, too. If it is suspended around the neck of an infant, it shall dispel all fear from them and relieve any vexations from evil spirits which afflict them.

To be of the greatest efficacy, this amulet should be set in a ring of iron, the metal of which should weigh twice as much as the carved stone.

If the figure of a standing eagle is fashioned out of etite[30] and set in a ring of lead, whoever wears it shall become popular and well-liked by all people. Animals will also become obedient to them.

The image of a ram together with a lion, carved out of any precious stone and set in a ring of silver, has the power of reconciling those who are in conflict, if they are touched by this ring.

To protect yourself from all harm, carve the astronomical sign of Capricorn into a carnelian (or in any other suitable stone), set it in a ring of silver, and carry it with you at all times. Then none of your foes will be able to harm you in the least, either physically or by their words; nor will any judge be able to pass an unjust sentence against you. You will prosper in all that you undertake, and secure for yourself the friendship and favor of many. Also, all spells and conjurations

---

30 A type of mythical stone believed to be found in the nests of eagles.

which are made against you shall be rendered ineffective, and no enemy—no matter how strong they are—will be able to stand against you in battle.

Here ends the tract of the ancient sage Chael on the potencies and virtues of amulets.

Tract III

The Amulets of
Thrice-Great Hermes

The fourth book of the *Liber Quadripartus* of Hermes Trismegistus[31] lists a number of powerful amulets, together with their effects and potencies.

The image of a tall man standing upright and holding an obolus[32] in one hand and a serpent in the other, with the sun over his head and a lion crouching at his feet, should be carved out of diadochus.[33] You should set this amulet in a ring made from lead, placing a little wormwood, mugwort, or the root of a fenugreek

---

31 Hermes Trismegistus was a legendary Hellenistic figure, identified with the Greek deity Hermes and/or the Egyptian deity Thoth. Many writings were attributed to him, which are mostly clearly pseudepigraphal and of Medieval or Renaissance origin. There are some, however (identified as the *Corpus Hermeticum*) which seem to be of genuine antiquity. These expound a form of mystical or gnostic Neo-Platonism.

32 A kind of ancient Greek coin.

33 A mythical precious stone resembling beryl.

plant underneath it. If you wear this ring or carry it with you, when you stand on the banks of a river, you shall be empowered to summon forth any aquatic spirits dwelling there, and compel them to answer your questions.

The figure of a standing man, holding a bushel of herbs at his throat (the said bushel having the thickness of a kidney, and being as long as a broadsword), should be carved from green jasper, to produce a useful and efficacious amulet. For such a figure will be able both to prevent fevers and to alleviate fevers from those suffering from them. If a practitioner of the medical arts carries it with them, it will greatly enhance their capacities in diagnosing illnesses, and prescribing the appropriate herbs, medicines and potions. It also helps in controlling hemorrhages and bleeding, and, when applied directly to a wound, can even stop the flow of blood immediately.[34]

A person who wears the image of a sea turtle, carved from coral and set in a ring of lead, will not be able to be harmed by anyone. Moreover, they will gain the affection and esteem of their seniors and masters.

---

34 This has a very close resemblance to one of the amulets described in the tract on the amulets of Thetel.

The figure of Aquarius [that is, a person carrying a vessel filled with water], sculpted from green jasper, will make whoever carries it prosperous in all matters of buying and selling. It will also cause merchants to turn to that person for advice, and profits to flow into their household.

[The next of the amulets of Hermes is] the likeness of a bird holding a leaf in its mouth. This bird should be looking at the head of a human being, who is looking back at the bird. If such an image is fashioned from pangonia[35] stone and set in gold, it will make the person who possesses it become wealthy and prosperous, and to be respected by all.

The figure of Jove—as a man sitting upon a throne with four legs—is an effective and useful amulet in obtaining one's desires. There should be four men standing before the seated figure of Jove, while he has his hands raised to the Heavens, and wears a crown upon his head. This image should be carved from jacinth, and set in a ring of gold. Any person who wears or carries such a ring, or has the imprint of such a ring impressed upon a

---

35 Any type of stone occurring in many-sided, imperfect crystalline formations (such as pyrite).

piece of wax (which can then be suspended around the neck), will obtain whatever they request from princes, kings, philosophers and scholars.

Another potent talisman is the image of a human being with the face of a lion and the feet of an eagle. There should be a dragon, with his tail extended, seated under the man's feet. The man should hold a rod or staff in his hand, with which he strikes the dragon's head. This design should be carved in crystal (or any other precious stone), and set in a ring of orichalcum,[36] with a little musk and amber placed under the amulet. Spirits will become obedient to the commands of anyone who wears such a ring, who will thus acquire very great powers indeed!

The form of a man seated upon an eagle and carrying a rod in his hand may be carved out of crystal, and set in a ring of bronze or copper. If anyone looks intently upon this ring before dawn on the day of the Sun,[37] they will be assured of overcoming all their foes and rivals. If a person looks upon it on the day of Jove,[38] they will emerge victorious from battle, and will find

---

36 An alloy of gold and copper, of a brightly gleaming appearance, but of lesser value than gold.

37 i.e. Sunday.

38 i.e. Thursday.

that all people will obey them without resistance. However, it behooves the one who wears this potent ring to dress in white garments, and to abstain from eating the flesh of doves and pigeons.

A figure of a man riding a horse, holding the reins in one hand and a bow in the other, and wearing a sword at his belt, should be sculpted from pyrite and then set in a ring of gold. Whoever wears such a ring will be victorious in battle, and there will be none who will be able to withstand them.

The image of a woman with long hair flowing over her bosom, looking lovingly upon a man who is coming towards her and making some sign of affection to her, may be carved from jacinth or crystal, and set in a ring of gold. A little amber, aloe and wormwood or mugwort should be inserted underneath the stone. Whoever wears such a ring will find that all people become obedient to them. Moreover, if you touch any woman with this ring, she will instantly fall in love with you. And if you place it under your head as you sleep, you shall see whatever you wish in your dreams.

Fashion from any type of red stone the figure of a man seated upon a fish, with a peacock perched on his head. If you place this amulet under a table, whoever eats at that table (provided they use their right hand to do so) will not feel satisfied.

The next image is the figure of a naked man, with a girl or maiden standing at his right, with her hair bound up around her head. The man is to hold his right hand above the neck of the girl and his left hand above her chest. He is looking at her, but she is looking at the ground. This scene may be carved from any variety of stone, and set in a ring of iron. A small portion of the tongue of a sparrow or hoopoe bird, some myrrh, some alum, and some human blood should be placed under the stone when it is being set in the ring. Whoever possesses such a ring will be invincible, and none shall be able to oppose them. Moreover, no wild animal will do them any harm.

If you make an imprint of this amulet by impressing it into red wax, it will be effective in preventing fits. And if you hold it at the throat of a dog, the animal shall refrain from barking.

The image of a man holding flowers in his hand, if sculpted from carnelian and placed in a ring of tin, will cause whomsoever you touch with it to become obedient to your every wish. To be effective, it should be made on either the day of the Moon[39] or the day of Venus,[40] at the fourth, eighth or twelfth hour.[41]

[Another amulet of notable potency] is the figure of a bearded man with a long face, a stooped posture and a supercilious expression, sitting on a plough between two bulls, and holding a vulture in his hand. This may be fashioned from stone [of any kind]. This device has the power of ensuring success in the planting of trees, in finding treasure, and in achieving victory in battle. It will also put to flight serpents, heal those suffering from fits, and dispel vexations caused by malevolent spirits. This amulet should be set in a ring of iron, and then [having been set thus] should be worn or carried about the person of its possessor.[42]

The figure of a man holding a scythe above his head, and standing on a crocodile, may be carved from any variety of stone. It should be set in a ring of lead, with a

---

39 I.e., Monday.

40 I.e., Friday.

41 These hours are determined by dividing the time from sunrise to sunset into twelve equal parts, and numbering accordingly.

42 This amulet is very similar in its design and properties to one described in the previous tract.

fragment of the root of a sea squill[43] placed underneath it. Any person who wears such a ring shall be kept safe from their enemies. If undertaking a journey, they will be protected from the attacks of thieves and robbers throughout their travels.

The figure of a man seated upon a dragon with a sword in his hand, carved out of amethyst, will cause spirits to obey the one who bears it, and will compel them to reveal the location of any hidden treasure. This amulet should be set in a ring of either lead or iron, and worn upon the finger.

The figure of a standing eagle, sculpted from etite[44] and set in a ring of lead, imparts to its bearer the ability to catch many fish. Furthermore, that person will not be harmed by any beast. In addition to this, they shall be well-liked by other people.[45]

---

43 A plant with a bulbous root, which grows in coastal areas (*Urginea maritima*).

44 A type of mythical stone believed to be found in the nests of eagles.

45 This amulet is identical in design to one described in the previous tract. The properties attributed to it there are also very similar.

The form of a man holding a palm branch in his hand, if fashioned from any variety of stone, will cause the person who bears it to be regarded with favor and friendship by princes and potentates.

Here ends the treatise of Thrice-Great Hermes on the potencies of stone amulets.

Tract IV

The Amulets of Thetel

Thetel,[46] that most ancient and wise teacher and physician, has declared that amulets may possess great and varied potencies when fashioned from the appropriate kinds of stone.

[One such powerful amulet Thetel describes is] the likeness of a human being, sculpted from jasper, and having a shield in his left hand and either an idol or some weapon of war in his right hand. In the place where the feet would normally be, there should be the forms of small vipers, and instead of a human head, there should be the head of either a rooster or a lion. Such an amulet ensures certain victory over one's enemies. It imparts immunity to poisons, and also has the effect of preventing hemorrhages or bleeding from any part of the body.

---

46 It seems that the person referred to here as Thetel is identical with Techellus, a legendary ancient Hebrew physician, referred to by Agrippa and Paracelsus.

The likeness of a human being with a bound bundle of herbs hanging from his neck, again if fashioned from a jasper stone, imparts to its bearer the power to discern and diagnose human diseases and infirmities with unfailing accuracy. It also prevents the loss of blood from the body. It is said that the legendary physician Galen possessed such an amulet, and it greatly assisted his capacity to diagnose his patients' maladies with assurance and confidence.[47]

A cross made from green jasper is said to liberate the person who possesses it from the peril of being submerged in water or drowned.

The form of a woman carrying a bird in one hand and a fish in the other, when carved out of chrysolite, is efficacious in procuring success in negotiations of all kinds.

---

47 Galen was an ancient Greek physician, of the second century BC.

A wolf carved out of jasper defends the person who possesses it against the cunning and deceitfulness of others. It also prevents that person from inadvertently or carelessly uttering any foolish or rash words.

The form of a deer made from jasper has the power to heal people from lunacy and frenzy.

If the figure of an emperor, standing upright with his head held high, is fashioned out of jasper, it shall render the person who bears it likeable and agreeable to all others. Thus it shall be that the person who possesses such an amulet will find that whatsoever they request of another, they shall be granted without any hesitation or delay.

The form of a maiden garbed in flowing vestments and holding in her hand a laurel, if sculpted from jasper, protects the one who bears it from submersion in water and drowning. It also guards its owner from being vexed by demonic entities. In addition, it shall make him or her more powerful and competent, rendering them fully capable of achieving whatever goals to which they may aspire.

A jasper amulet in the form of a man having in his hand a palm branch imparts to the person who bears it the ability to gain favor with rulers and authorities.

Thus wrote the venerable philosopher and physician Thetel on the mystical powers of amulets.

The Amulets of
King Solomon the Wise

An ancient book was once discovered in the deserts by some wandering Israelites. Because many works written by Solomon were found to be contained in this book,[48] they attributed the authorship of the entire volume to Solomon. The title of one of the tracts contained therein is 'Stone Amulets, in accordance with Thy Name, O God, and according to the course of the stars'.

[The first amulet in this treatise of Solomon is] the figure of a man with a short neck and a large beard, seated upon a plough, and with four [smaller] men lying at his neck. He should be holding in one hand a vulture, and in the other hand a fox. If a person wears such an image around their neck, they shall be

---

48 The biblical books of Proverbs, Ecclesiastes, Song of Songs, and Wisdom are all traditionally attributed to Solomon, as well as innumerable pseudepigraphical tracts.

successful in all plantings and sowings they undertake, and also succeed in finding hidden treasures.

If you wish to experience for yourself the effectiveness of this amulet, wrap it in some pure, undyed, black wool, together with a little chaff of wheat. Then place it under your head as you sleep, and you will see in your dreams any hidden treasures which may be in the surrounding region.

This amulet also has the power to heal all ailments of beasts, if they are given to drink some water in which it has been washed.[49]

The image of a man having a shield suspended from his neck, a helmet on his head, and holding a sword upright, should be carved from green jasper. The man in the figure is also to be treading a serpent under his feet. If you wear such an amulet around your neck, you will not fear any enemy. You will be victorious in all conflicts, especially those of a military nature. To be most effective, the carving should be set in bronze or copper.

The likeness of a horse carrying a crocodile upon its back, carved from white jasper, renders its possessor well-liked, both by human beings and by animals.

49 This amulet and its properties are identical to the first one described in the tract attributed to Chael.

Another powerful amulet is the figure of a seated man with his eyes directed upwards, with a woman standing before him, with long hair hanging to her thighs. This should be fashioned from carnelian. It renders all persons, both male and female, obedient to the one who bears it. It ought to be set in a ring of gold, the weight of the metal being equal to the weight of the stone. When the stone is being set into this ring, a little hedgenettle and amber should be placed beneath it.

The image of a horse, foaming at the mouth, and with a man holding a scepter in his hand seated upon his back, carved out of amethyst, brings much profit to the person who possesses it. For all who carry it shall find that princes and rulers become instantly compliant to their wishes. It ought to be set in gold or silver, the metal of the setting weighing twice as much as the stone.

The image of the head of a man with a long beard and a little blood on his neck, if carved from diamond, will confer to anyone who possesses it victory and courage. It will also preserve their body from wounds, and help them attain favor with rulers.

The figure of a person playing a musical instrument, fashioned out of sapphire, has the property of rendering the person who carries it extremely pleasing to all whom they encounter.

The likeness of a rooster, or of three hens,[50] made from an agate, will make the person who possesses it pleasing in the sight of both God and mortals.

The form of a lion fashioned from granite brings to the one who bears it riches and honors. It makes its possessor joyful, and dispels all traces of melancholy from the heart.

The figure of a deer or a dove carved from an onyx bestows upon the one who carries it strength and fortitude against all demonic entities.

---

50 The Latin text here in the 1732 edition is '*trium puellarum*', meaning 'of three girls'. However, it seems likely that this is typographical or scribal error, and that '*trium pullarum*' ('three chicks/three hens') is actually intended.

The image of a merchant carrying his merchandise (as if going to the market to sell it) will secure victory and riches for its possessor, and relieve anxiety. It should be carved from an emerald. The form of a man seated beneath a centurion, again carved from an emerald, has a similar effect.

An amulet of a bull or an ox made from lodestone ensures a safe journey for the one who carries it. It also confers protection against all spells and incantations.

The form of either a horse or a wolf, carved from jasper, has the power to dispel fevers and to assist the clotting of blood.

The form of a crowned man, made from a topaz, will render the person who bears it good and upright, and cause them to be beloved by both God and mortals. In addition, it will lead them to acquire honors and dignities.

The figure of an armed man, with a sword in his hand, and carved from either sard or amethyst, improves and perfects the faculty of memory in the person who bears it. It also imparts to them prudence and wisdom.

The form of a deer or a billy-goat made from chalcedony will bestow upon its owner an increase in wealth. In order to do this, the amulet should be locked up in the chest in which one keeps one's money and treasures.

A person who carries the form of a rabbit made of jasper will not be harmed by any demons.

A lobster carved out of beryl has the effect of reconciling persons who are in conflict, and of promoting or restoring love between married couples.

The night heron is the bird sacred to Pallas Athena, the goddess of wisdom. For this reason, if the image of a night heron is carved from stone, it produces an increase in erudition in the person who possesses it. It will also render them more eloquent in their speech.

The image of a peacock, fashioned from any suitable stone, will cause the person who carries it to acquire riches.

The figure of a man killing a lion (or any other dangerous beast or monster) with a sword, will render its possessor astute, victorious and popular.

The image of a man holding a laurel or palm branch in his right hand will make the one who carries it attain victory in battle and in legal disputes. It will also make them popular and powerful within their region.

An image of a man with wings, who tramples a serpent under his feet whilst holding the head of the same serpent in his hand, will make anyone who carries it become rich, wise, and well-liked by all.

Another amulet which is effective in obtaining riches is the form of an ant holding an ear of grain, or a single grain. It may be sculpted from any variety of stone.

The image of a rooster holding a crown or a belt in its beak bestows on the one who possesses it certain victory in any duel in which they partake. This is especially so if the duel takes place at the hour of cock-crow.

If you fashion the figure of a man with the head of an ox and the feet of an eagle out of a gemstone of any kind, and then impress it into soft wax, no person will ever speak ill about you.[51]

[Translator's note: There follows here a number of further amulets, but these are identical to ones described previously.]

Here ends the tract on stone amulets, attributed to the sagacious King Solomon.

---

51 This amulet and its effect is almost identical to one in the tract attributed to Chael; however, that version omits mention of impressing the carving into wax. The present description does not prescribe carrying either the figure or its wax impression. This may imply that the simple act of applying the figure to the wax is sufficient to benefit from its particular power.

An Exposition of the Reasons

One may well enquire as to the reason why various engraved rings and amulets fashioned from certain stones or metals possess their particular powers and potencies, as described in the preceding tracts. It is to be noted that the reason is *not* any quality of the materials from which they are made, nor does it originate from some property arising from the totality of their form and substance. Rather the reason is Divine, or magical. This indicates that it originates from some more sublime and hidden Cause, which may be appropriately termed a spiritual bond or conduit. For by the mediation of this hidden Cause, the physical and spiritual realms (which are far removed from each other in substance and nature) are brought into connection. This is analogous to the unseen and mysterious force by which a magnet attracts iron, or by which the sunflower follows the movements of the sun.

[It is pertinent to provide here a number of examples of the workings of this unseen and mystic connection, whereby spiritual forces—represented by the planetary powers—exercise their influence via physical objects, colors, flavors and locations.

As our first case, we may consider the planet Mercury.][52] With this invisible and mystical force—this spiritual bond or conduit—mediating and intervening, the energy of the planet Mercury is powerfully present in quicksilver. In this form, it is efficacious in sharpening the memory and cognitive faculties. But this same supernatural and planetary power is transmitted also through the form of electrum, which [unlike quicksilver] is a solid substance.[53] When present in this latter form, it has the reverse effect to that of quicksilver, and serves rather to debilitate and impair the same mental faculties. The influence of the planet Mercury is associated with all mixed and combined colors and flavors. Its effects are found to be strongest in the lands of Egypt, Greece, Flanders and Cilicia.

Through the mediation of this same unseen force or connection, the power of the Moon is present both in silver and in glass. The same lunar energy is also

---

52 The discussion which follows, of the planetary powers and their connection with various minerals, colors and physical forms and locations, is apparently intended to demonstrate the connection between spiritual and physical realities.

53 Electrum is a naturally occurring alloy of gold and silver. The equation of it with Mercury is not to be understood in terms of element in contemporary chemistry, but rather the spiritual force or energy represented in the planet Mercury.

active in the human cerebrum, as well as in the left eye of men, and the right eye of women. It is manifested through the colors of radiant white, and cerulean blue, and in any ashen hue. It is associated with a salty flavor, and often manifests a crystalline form. The Moon's energy is found to be most potent in the northerly regions, including Flanders, Holland, Zealand,[54] and Denmark.

The force of the planet Saturn is strongly present in lead. It is active also in the right ear, the spleen, and the bones. It is associated with the colors of black, dark purple, and leaden gray. This spiritual force is characterized by a bitter flavor. It is often active in black stones concealed in shadowy places, and is especially powerful in the regions of Saxony and Styria.[55]

[By the same mystical connection,] the potency and activity of the planet Jupiter is to be found in tin. In the human body, it is active in the lungs, ribs, wrists, semen, and the left ear. It is associated with the colors of bright yellow, purple, gold, and verdant green; and the gemstones emerald, sapphire, and amethyst. In taste, it is sweet. It is most potent in the regions of the Nordic lands, as well as Babylon, Persia, Hungary, and Spain.

The golden and majestic Sun exercises its noble and vivifying influence through the heart, the arteries, the right eye, and the right side of the body. Its potency is expressed in the aureate color of gold, the bright

---

54 A large island in the Danish straits.

55 A region of Austria.

purple of the crocus flower, various reddish tints, and the radiant violet of the hyacinth. It is associated with a sharp and somewhat bitter flavor, and with a pleasant, but not overpowering, fragrance. The spiritual force of the Sun tends to be most active in the Oriental regions.

The war-like potency of Mars is powerfully present in iron, and is associated with the left ear, the gall bladder and the kidneys. The jasper stone also serves as a conduit to its energy. It is associated with a sharp, bitter, and acrid taste. The power of Mars is particularly active and effective in the regions of Sarmatia,[56] Getulia,[57] Lombardy[58] and Gotland.[59]

The energy of Venus is transmitted by the metal copper, and is strongly active in mirrored surfaces of all varieties. Its potency works through the womb, the kidneys, the breast, the throat, the genitals, and the liver. It is associated with the color white, and possesses a flavor that is both oily and sweet. Pearls, sapphire and garnets all serve as conduits to its potency and effects. The influence of Venus is particularly prevalent in Austria, Arabia, Campania,[60] Poland, and Switzerland.

---

56 A region of modern-day Iran.

57 A region in northern Africa, inhabited by the Berbers.

58 In Italy.

59 A region of Sweden.

60 A region in south-west Italy.

Now, to seek the cause of these hidden influences in the qualities, nature, or even the totality of substance for any of the examples given above is not only absurd but even ridiculous. For the forces which are active and the powers which are at work are not of a corporeal nature, and originate from a realm which is not physical.[61] Therefore no precise account or measure of these processes can be given with reference to those things which are perceptible by, and comprehensible to, the corporeal senses, or the intellect which is informed by them. In these matters, ambitious and presumptuous arguments based on words alone and inane rational demonstrations must surely and inevitably fail!

To give an example of this, if someone seeks to provide a physical or rational explanation for the appearance of white roses, they may attempt to them ascribe to some 'cold humor' [62] within the rose bush. Yet how will they then account for precisely the same

---

61 At this stage, the realm of the Heavens which contained the planets was understood not to consist of 'matter' of the same nature and quality as that found on earth, but a more rarified and spiritual substance or material. Furthermore, the spiritual powers represented by the planets were not absolutely identified with the visible planets themselves, but neither absolutely distinct from them. Hence, there was understood to be a continuum between material and spiritual, and spatial and non-spatial, realities.

62 Living things (including plants, animals and human beings) were believed to possess different 'humors' (which could be hot or cold, and wet or dry). These humors were believed both to reflect and to determine their character and properties.

species of bush producing red roses? Or perhaps a person may naively claim that the chicory plant produces milky sap, because it is of a cold humor. Yet how then will they account for a plant like the cactus, which is very clearly of a hot humor, but which produces exactly the same type of milky sap as the chicory? Or, to give another example, you may say that the aloe plant has a bitter flavor, because of its warm humor. Yet opium also has an extremely bitter taste; but it can serve as a lethal poison precisely because of its exceptionally *cold* humor.

Even in such simple matters as these, it is clear that attempted rational explanations can never suffice to account for these various and diverse phenomena. And if no satisfactory rational explanations can be provided for the things of nature, does it not behoove us to acknowledge humbly that such things reflect the planning and dispositions of some all-wise Creator, whose ways entirely transcend our own, and whose wisdom and methods are beyond our comprehension?

How vain is it, then, to demand rational explanations for the connections between common material forms and mystical spiritual energies! Such connections may be observed, documented and catalogued, but they are wholly beyond our capacity to explain.

Of course, the use of amulets and images can easily degenerate to the level of a mere empty superstition, when people fail to recognize that whatever effects and powers they possess are solely the result of the will and wisdom of the supreme Creator. Many foolishly imagine, instead, that such devices are efficacious in and of themselves. Yet this is clearly not the case at all.

Let us, then, not be overly hasty to dismiss the wisdom given to us regarding these devices and images by the ancient sages. These ancient sages have carefully observed through long experience that certain images and amulets possess particular powers, as determined by the unseen dispositions of the Divine will. Indeed, there is, ultimately, no power in Heaven or on earth except for that which originates from an omnipotent and supreme Creator. Thus medicinal herbs, which are corporeal bodies, have the power to heal. Yet, in the final analysis, this power comes not from the herbs themselves, but from God Himself. And certain verbal incantations, which are incorporeal, also have the power to heal; which similarly comes from the same unseen Supreme Spirit.

Therefore those methods and devices—such as magical amulets—whose workings transcend the narrow limits of physical observation or rational explanation, should neither be condemned nor derided. For the will of the unseen Creator, who is both all-wise and infinitely benevolent, has disposed it thus, and manifests itself in their remarkable properties and effects.

Bibliotheca Necromantica

The passage given below is a translation of
the listing of books on magic, necromancy,
divination, astrology, and other related fields,
compiled by Trithemius and included in his
Antipalus Maleficiorum (Book I, Chapter 3).[63]
It is not entirely clear whether his ostensible
condemnation of these books is merely for
the sake of appearances, but it is clear that
Trithemius was intimately familiar with the
works which he describes, and was an avid
collector of such arcane and esoteric volumes.
The numberings in the text are editorial
additions, included for the sake of reference.

---

63 Johannes Trithemius, *Antipalus Maleficiorum* (Mainz:
Balthasar Lippius, 1605), pp. 290–301. The text (without
translation) is also reproduced in Paola Zambelli, *White
Magic, Black Magic in the European Renaissance: From Ficino, Pico,
Della Porta to Trithemius, Agrippa, Bruno* (Leiden: Brill, 2007),
pp. 102–107.

1. There is a volume entitled the *Lesser Key of Solomon,*[64] which begins: 'Remember, my son Rehoboam...' But Solomon, the venerable king of Jerusalem, certainly neither composed nor ever saw this volume, although it bears his name. And what does it contain except vain, foolish, counterfeit and openly false things? It promises all things, but delivers nothing to those who use it—except for deception, harm to their consciences, and the enslavement of their souls to demons. Whoever wrote this book was clearly woefully uneducated, and a deserter of the Christian religion. For the language is entirely ungrammatical, and its pages filled with outlandish demonic characters and names.

2. There is also a *Book of Offices,* which begins, 'Many wise persons have written...' It is overflowing with falsehoods, as no-one who has even a mediocre education will fail to recognize. And what wise person is able to hear without laughing the way in which it distinguishes demons into four ranks—emperors, kings, dukes, marquises and counts? And who would seriously believe (as is claimed in this book) that holy men, such as Adam, Seth, Noah, Terah, Abraham, Moses, David,

---

64 Trithemius gives the word for 'small key' in its plural form, *'claviculae'*. However, as the genitive and nominative plural forms of the word are identical, he may mean 'Book *of* the Small Key'. The title given above is the one in customary use today.

Solomon, Ezekiel, Daniel and the other ancient patriarchs and prophets, applied their efforts to these demonic arts and foul superstitions? And who could ever believe such wise and holy people to have composed kabbalistic tables, as certain accursed people try to assert?

3. There is another volume, consisting of ten books, which begins: 'The progress of the Divine condition...' The author identifies himself as Job of Arabia. Such marvels as can scarcely be believed are promised in this book through the services and arts of demons. These are not only vain and foolish, but often patently impossible. The compiler of this book imitates the author of the *Picatrix* [described next] in many of its ideas, figures and spells.

4. *Picatrix* composed a great volume in four books,[65] which begins thus: 'As a wise person has once said, what we ought to do...' This work is said to have been compiled from some 240 books of ancient sages, and to have been translated from Arabic into Latin in the year of our Lord 1256. It contains many frivolous, superstitious, and diabolical things, expressed in plain and unadorned language; although there are many [valid] elements of natural science mixed in as

---

65 This book is normally identified by the title *Picatrix*, although Trithemius gives this is as the name of its author or compiler.

well. It offers prayers to the spirits of the planets, and describes images in magical rings, and various other mystical figurations. All of these are rightly condemned by Holy Mother Church as unlawful and superstitious.

5. There is also a work comprising seven books, which is called *Sepher Razielis.* It begins thus: 'I, Solomon, said, 'Glory, praise and highest honor be to the Lord, the Creator of all things!''It speaks much about spirits and promises great things, but is replete with vanity and superstition.

6. Then there is the *Book of Hermes,* which is also called the *Angelic Book* or the *Book of Angels,* or the *Hidden Book composed by Three Angels, before the Flood.* It begins thus: 'This is a great and secret book...' It contains false and counterfeit names of twelve ranks of angels, under the twenty-eight houses of the Moon and the twelve signs of the Zodiac. Indeed, whatever human curiosity and ambition is able to dare to desire, this book promises, according to the usual manner of such works!

7. There is the book entitled the *Purities of God.* It claims to have been revealed to Adam (when he was repenting for his sins), by the angel Raziel. It matches the previously mentioned work [the *Book of Hermes*] in many respects. The text of this book begins thus: 'Adam was expelled from Paradise...' It is a totally inane work, filled with superstitions

and unknown names. It contains invocations and figures, and promises many strange and even impossible things.

8. Next, there is a work which is called the *Book of the Perfection of Saturn*, which commences: 'Abel, the son of Adam, found this book...' What foolish and bold presumption it is of these wretches, who are not afraid to ascribe these superstitions even to the holy and innocent Abel!

9. There is another and most pestiferous work, called the *Book of Four Kings*, after the number of demons it invokes. The beginning of its text varies [in the different versions in circulation], but some manuscripts commence thus: 'Of the art of magic, whoever...' In other copies, the text begins differently. There are some who dare to ascribe this accursed volume to the holy martyr, St. Cyprian.[66] Reading this book should be strictly forbidden—even, indeed, under pain of the punishment of death!

10. There is a book entitled the *Art of Calculation of Virgil*, which promises a method whereby anyone may

---

66 St. Cyprian of Antioch, venerated as the patron saint of magicians and sorcerers, who was martyred together with St. Justina during the Diocletian persecutions in the early fourth century. See Alexander Cummins, *The Art of Cyprian's Mirror of Four Kings: An Early Modern Experiment of Cyprianic Conjuration* (West Yorkshire: Hadean Press, 2021).

calculate the names and characters of spirits, both beneficent and baleful. It contains many spells and demonic characters, and begins thus: 'Never did I become tired or exhausted with calculation...' One may be fully confident that Virgil himself never even saw this book, as it claims!

11. There is also a book ascribed to Simon Magus, which begins: 'Once when I was in Judea...' Everything it contains is futile, superstitious, counterfeit and mindless. It promises many things through demons, but these promises are nothing other than mendacious deceptions, designed to prey upon the minds of the curious.

12. Next, there is a volume ascribed to a certain Rupert (of whom I know nothing), containing four books, and named the *Treasury of Spirits*. Using symbols and names of demons, it promises (with much audacity) to be able to procure the obedience of evil spirits, whenever they are summoned into a magical circle. It begins: 'I, Rupert of Lombardy...' Other copies of this work commence differently, namely: 'Here begins the tract on necromancy, with notes...'

13. Then, there is the *Book of Spiritual Works*, which is attributed to the philosopher Aristotle. It commences: 'To every people, there are seven climates...' It contains some [sound] material pertaining to astronomy, but this is mixed up

with futile and foolish invocations of demons. Nevertheless, this work does exhibit considerable effort, learning, and labor.

14. There is a sizeable volume, which is called the *Flower of Flowers*, and divided into many books. It contains various invocations, names and symbols of demons. Many of its pernicious and diabolic experiments are to be utterly condemned, as being entirely contrary to the Christian religion. It begins thus: 'The flower of flowers, and the experience of all...'

15. Pertaining to these same most vain superstitions is the *Book of Almadel*, attributed to Solomon. Its text begins: 'We have discovered the illumination of the Holy Spirit...' Many foul and contemptible falsehoods are conveyed in it. These are all demonic, and deservedly condemned by the Church of God.

16. Next, there is an entirely fictitious book, ascribed to Enoch. It contains a far-fetched narration concerning fifteen stars, and their corresponding herbs, figures and stones. Through this knowledge, it promises many strange and outlandish things (as do other books of this type). The stupidity of its author is demonstrated from the very beginning of the work, which commences thus: 'I, Enoch, one of the four prophets and philosophers, offer grace to the Messiah who is to come after me...'

17. The *Book of the Rings of the Seven Planets* is attributed to Messala,[67] and begins thus: 'When you wish to work...' Everything it contains is utterly vain and superstitious, and to be avoided by Christians.

18. There is another work, entitled the *Book of the Four Rings of Solomon.* The most wicked people and deluded conjurers of demons greatly delight in this nefarious volume! Nevertheless, it contains nothing but inane superstitions. It commences thus: 'There were four rings possessed by Idaea'[68]

19. The book entitled the *Mirror of Joseph* promises visions through a particular type of personal mirror. Its text commences: 'If you wish to see all things...'

20. There is another treatise which should be mentioned here, called the *Mirror of Alexander the Great, King of the Macedonians.* It has been invented and composed with similar malignity, and begins thus: 'Of this great secret...'

21. The book of the *Secrets of Hermes of Spain* begins: 'Whoever wishes to converse with spirits...' It is a work which is similarly vain, superstitious and

---

67 Possibly Marcus Silius Messala, a Roman senator of the third century.

68 Idaea (or Jedidiah) was one of several alternative names for Solomon. See 2 Samuel 12:25.

diabolical, and entirely filled with demonic figures and conjurations.

22. The work entitled *Summa Magicae* is a large tome, divided into a great many books, and written by a certain Beringarius Ganellus.[69] It commences thus: 'Magic is the science of compelling spirits, both maleficent and benign, through the name of God...' O good Lord, how very foolish, frivolous and fatuous is this author to expend his efforts compiling all this damnable material into one compendium, thus showing himself to be a soldier of the demons rather than a fighter for God! Some persons assert that this, or a similar, compilation was made by a certain Tozigeus, whom others call Toez the Greek.[70] That work matches closely and confirms all the superstitions [contained in the *Summa Magicae*, attributed to the said Ganellus].

---

69 A Catalan magician of the fourteenth century. The text of Trithemius has the word *Ungario* ('Hungarian') in place of the name *Beringario*, but this is almost certainly an error.

70 This Tozigeus or Toez the Greek was supposedly a student of Solomon. If it is read as 'Thoth the Greek', it may be intended to be an alternative appellation for Hermes Trismegistus.

23. There is a tract written by a certain Michael Scotus,[71] in which knowledge of all things is promised, through the instruction of the devil. But there is nothing in it which is not superstitious and diabolical. It begins: 'If you wish to have, through the spirit...'

24. There is another book, which commences: 'Before you begin...' The person who wrote it fraudulently attributes it to [St] Albert [the Great].[72] Following the custom of books of this type, it offers many inane formulae for summoning demons.

25. Another book falsely attributed to the same learned Albert is entitled *On Invisibility*. This is absolutely full of superstitions of the most contemptible

---

71 A thirteen-century British mathematician and scholar, who also wrote on chiromancy, alchemy and astrology. This remarkable and curious text is to be found in Brian Johnson, *Necromancy in the Medici Library: An Edition and Translation of Excerpts from Biblioteca Medicea Laurenziana, MS Plut. 89 sup. 38* (West Yorkshire: Hadean Press, 2020), 61–75. That text begins, '*Si volueris per demones habere*', whereas the version cited by Trithemius here commences, '*Si volueris per spiritum habere*'.

72 St. Albert the Great, the teacher of St. Thomas Aquinas, was regarded as the most learned man of his time. His apparently authentic writings include works on the mystical and medicinal properties of minerals, plants and animals. See, for example, St. Albert the Great, *Liber Secretorum Alberti Magni de Virtutibus Herbarum, Lapidum et Animalium* (Cologne: Joannes Gymicus, 1555).

variety. The text commences: 'I adjure you, O three Princes!'

The accursed dealers in the occult falsely ascribe many other volumes of necromancy, not only to Albert the Great, but also to various other saints and doctors of the Church. Of course, such innocent and devout people never even thought about these matters! Rather, it seems to me that Albert, as a most holy and erudite man, would have firmly condemned such books.

26. There is a book which bears the title the *Elucidation of Necromancy*, attributed to Peter of Abano, a physician from Padua, known as 'the Conciliator'.[73] Concerning this Peter de Abano, many far-fetched things are said. The present book contains nothing sound at all, but its material is totally vain and superstitious. It presents a multitude of concocted names of spirits and formulae for summoning demons, for each year, month, day and hour. The text begins thus: 'Many experimenters, in different ways...' There are many other volumes ascribed to this same Peter of Abano, whoever the real author may actually be.

---

73 Peter of Abano was an Italian philosopher, physician and astrologer of the thirteenth and fourteenth centuries. The book referred to here is commonly known by the title of the *Heptameron*.

27. There is a certain perfidious treatise, overflowing with inanity, whose author is uncertain. It is called the *Secret of the Philosophers*, and begins: 'Here commences the great secret...' This work contains details of various [supposed] operations of demons.

28. Similar to this is the book which begins: '*Schemhamphoras*,[74] as the teachers say, is a name which is to be feared...' The name of the author is not given, and the whole work is purely fanciful invention. The author of the work (evidently a most vain person) makes counterfeit claims based on purported ancient documents, and proposes these as a means of summoning spirits.

29. There is another book attributed to Solomon, which is called *Lamen*. This work promises knowledge of all things, through the services of spirits. It begins thus: 'Solomon, the most wise king...'

30. There is a certain book on the formation of the names and symbols of evil spirits, which is similarly futile and superstitious. I have not been able to discover the name of the author of this work. It commences thus: 'An experiment for gaining knowledge...'

---

74 A hidden, kabbalistic name for God.

31. The book entitled *Rubeus* deals with the various arts and operations of demons. It is totally inane and diabolical, fraudulent, and very similar to the *Book of Offices.*[75] Its text opens with: 'This is given…'

32. There is a certain book falsely attributed to Albert the Great, to which its ill-educated author has given the title *The Secret of Albert*. It promises the achievement of familiarity with a certain malign spirit, and begins: 'In the name of the Father, the Son and the Spirit…'

33. The tract entitled *On the Work of Spirits* is attributed to Solomon. It commences: 'In this book is the secret of all the arts…'

34. There is also a volume bearing the title *The Chain of Spirits*. It contains many spells and conjurations, through which misguided and lost persons believe themselves to be able to constrain demons to obey their behests. This book begins: 'Concerning the chain of spirits, it is not fitting to remain silent…'

35. The *Book of the Pentacles of Solomon* is another work falsely attributed to that ancient king and philosopher. It features conjurations of demons, descriptions of pentacles, and many

---

75 See No. 2 in this catalogue.

other similarly vain devices. It commences: 'The method and technique of forming pentacles...'[76]

36. There is another book of Torzigeus,[77] entitled *On the Stations for the Worship of Venus*. It promises very much, but is completely superstitious and inane. It begins: 'The commemoration of histories...'

37. Another work by the same author bears the title *The Four Mirrors*. It commences thus: 'Observe Venus as it comes to the Pleaides...'

38. There is yet another book by this same Totzgraecus (also known as Tozigaeus, as some prefer it), with the title *On the Image of Venus*. The text of this volume commences: 'Observe Venus when it enters into Taurus...' As has been said above of his other writings, there are a great many inane things to be found here.

39. The tract *On the Nine Pentacles for the Summoning of Demons* is, like many other similar works, falsely attributed to Solomon. It is totally vain and superstitious, beginning thus: 'This place gives a warning, as we have said...'

---

76 Clear illustrations of many of these pentacles attributed to Solomon, together with transcriptions and translations of their pertinent texts, may be found in S. Aldarnay, *The Pentacles of Solomon* (West Yorkshire: Hadean Press, 2021).

77 Trithemius evidently means the same person, identified as 'Tozigeus' or 'Toez the Greek', in item No. 22.

40. Another book [attributed to] the same author is *On the Three Figures of Spirits,* which commences: 'There are, concerning celestial things...'

41. There is a book supposedly written by Muhammed, entitled *Of the Seven Names,* which begins: 'Muhammed, son of Abosen...'

42. Another work, attributed to the same author, begins: 'These are the fifteen names...' The title of this book is *Of the Fifteen Names.*

43. There exists a volume entitled *The Head of Saturn,* pertaining to necromancy and the conjuration of spirits. It is manifestly superstitious, and begins thus: 'This most secret thing...'

Those who practice necromancy speak of innumerable other books and treatises, attributed to a diversity of authors. Truly, such books [and their pseudepigraphical attributions] are all witnesses to the madness of these impious persons! To mention all the titles of these works and the names of their imagined authors would be an endeavor both long and tedious.

For a vast quantity of tracts are ascribed to Solomon (which we shall refrain from mentioning), and similarly to Hermes, Balaam, Raziel, Aristotle, Plato, Zoroaster, Roger Bacon (an English [Franciscan friar]), Rupert of Lombardy, Peter of Albano (a Paduan physician), Artephius,[78] Virgil, Thabit ibn Qurra, and a veritable multitude of others. [...] All of these books on necromancy are replete with vanities and deceptions, falsely presented under the names of venerable and reputable authors. They are written to ensnare curious people, through the opaque obfuscations, tenebrous turpitudes, and nebulous nullities with which they so profusely abound. [...]

But despite this, St. Albert the Great, in his noble opusculum on the two wisdoms entitled *The Mirror*, counsels that these volumes should be diligently conserved, saying:

Concerning these necromantic treatises, it seems to me that they ought now to be preserved, rather than destroyed. For the time is indeed drawing nigh—for reasons which it behooves me to pass over in silence—when it will be very useful for such books to be carefully read and studied... [79]

---

78 A twelfth-century alchemist.

79 The book referred to here is one of the genuine works of Albert, and the quote presented by Trithemius is almost an exact match with the text found in reliable scholarly editions of Albert's work. See St. Albert the Great, 'Speculum Astronomiae', in *B. Alberti Magni Opera omnia, Volume 10* (Paris: Ludovicum Vivès, 1891), p. 650. The description of the book as being 'on the two wisdoms' is a reference to Albert's division of astronomy into two separate systems of knowledge (theoretical and practical).

Bibliography

St. Albert the Great, *Liber Secretorum Alberti Magni de Virtutibus Herbarum, Lapidum et Animalium* (Cologne: Joannes Gymicus, 1555)

St. Albert the Great, 'Speculum Astronomiae', in *B. Alberti Magni Opera Omnia, Tomus X* (Paris: Ludovicum Vivès, 1891), pp. 629-650

Aldarnay, S., *The Pentacles of Solomon* (West Yorkshire: Hadean Press, 2021)

Cummins, Alexander, *The Art of Cyprian's Mirror of Four Kings: An Early Modern Experiment of Cyprianic Conjuration* (West Yorkshire: Hadean Press, 2021)

Duraclus, Johannes, 'Pinax sive Index Lucubrationum Joannis Trithemii, in Trithemius, Johannes, *Libri Polygraphiae VI* (Cologne: Johannes Birkmann and Werner Richwin, 1564), pp. 4-13

Heidel, Wolfgang Ernst, 'Epistola Dedicatoria Damiano Hartardo', in Trithemius, Johannes, *Steganographia Vindicata, Reserata et Illustrata* (Nuremberg: Johannes Friedrich Rüdiger, 1721)

Heidel, Wolfgang Ernst, 'Vita Joannis Trithemii', in Trithemius, Johannes, *Steganographia Vindicata, Reserata et Illustrata* (Nuremberg: Johannes Friedrich Rüdiger, 1721), pp. 1-42

Johnson, Brian, *Necromancy in the Medici Library: An Edition and Translation of Excerpts from Biblioteca Medicea Laurenziana, MS Plut. 89 sup. 38* (West Yorkshire: Hadean Press, 2020)

Jung, C.G., *The Archetypes and the Collective Unconscious*, trans. by R.F.C. Hull (London: Routledge, 2014)

Trithemius, Johannes, *Antwort auff acht Fragstuck* (Ingolstadt: Alexander and Samuel Weissenhorn, 1555)

Trithemius, Johannes, *Antipalus Maleficiorum* (Mainz: Balthasar Lippius, 1605)

Trithemius, Johannes, 'Chronicon Monasterii Sancti Jacobi', in Trithemius, Johannes, *Opera Pia et Spirituales* (Mainz: Johannes Albinus, 1605), pp. 1-17

Trithemius, Johannes, 'Orationes ad Sanctos', in *Paralipomena Opusculorum Petri Blesensis, et Joannis Trithemii, Aliorumque Nuper in Typographeo Moguntino Editorum* (Mainz: Balthasar Lippius, 1605), pp. 734-776

Trithemius, Johannes, *Veterum Sophorum Sigilla et Imagines Magicae* (Herrnstadt: Friedrich Roth-Scholtz, 1732)

Zambelli, Paola, *White Magic, Black Magic in the European Renaissance: From Ficino, Pico, Della Porta to Trithemius, Agrippa, Bruno* (Leiden: Brill, 2007)

9 781914 166433